Deborah and J

Deborah

Jael

Barak

King Jabin

Sisera

 First edition, published in the United Kingdom by Onwards and Upwards Publishers Ltd. (2020).

is mean!
KiNG JaBiN

A long time ago,
in a far-away land,
the Israelites lived –
but not as they'd planned.
Their king was called Jabin,
and he wasn't kind;
oh, he was the cruellest
king you could find!
He was mean, he was violent,
he caused many tears,
and he ruled over Israel
for twenty odd years.

We've had enough!
King Jabin
is mean!

The Israelites found it
so hard and so tough,
that they called out to God,
saying, "We've had enough!"
So God made a plan,
and the plan was good –
He knew it would work,
He knew that it would.
When God makes a plan,
He uses His friends,
So God used Deborah
to make amends.

Now Deborah was wise
and Deborah was strong.
Under a tree she would
sit all day long;
the people would come
and they'd ask her advice.
She'd tell them the right thing
to do in a trice.

So now that
the Israelites
needed a plan,
it was Deborah
that God sent
to rescue the clan.
She ordered Barak
to take 10,000 men,
to gather them all
at Mount Tabor, and then
Jabin's strong army
would make quite a din,
but God would make sure
that Barak's men would win!

Barak didn't want to
do this on his own.
He said, "Please come with me,
so I'm not alone."
Deborah said, "Fine,
but you won't get the glory.
There'll be quite a different
end to this story."
Now Deborah was wise
and Deborah was brave.
She went with Barak,
her people to save.

But Sisera, who was
  King Jabin's commander
had heard they were coming
  to fight and to plunder.
He gathered his chariots,
  called every soldier;
they marched and they marched,
  getting closer and bolder.
But God had a plan,
  and the plan was good –
He knew it would work,
  He knew that it would.
He'd rescue His people
  through Deborah, His friend.
Everything would turn out
  right in the end.

Deborah said, "Go!
God has gone right ahead –
He's given you victory –
so no need for dread!"
Barak was determined,
and he took his men
to Mount Tabor, attacking
and fighting – but then
Sisera started
to get so confused;
his chariots and warriors
were, oh, so bemused.

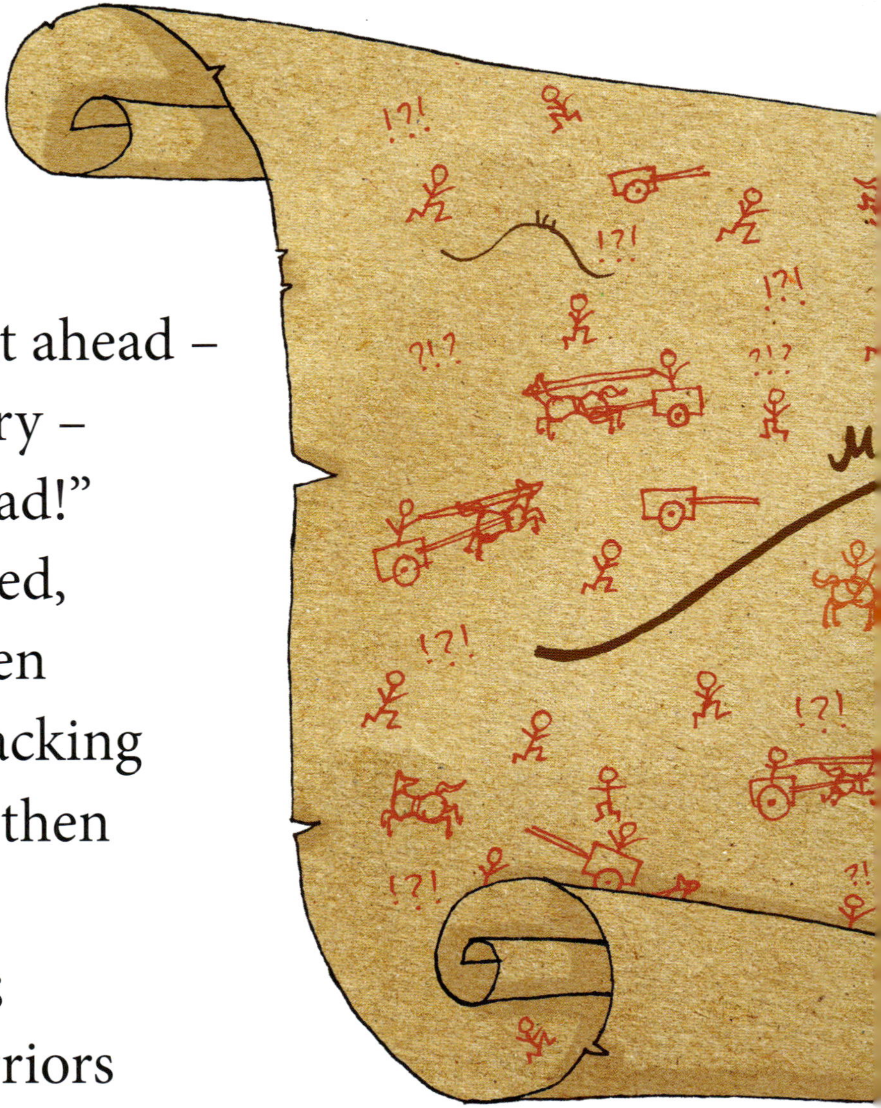

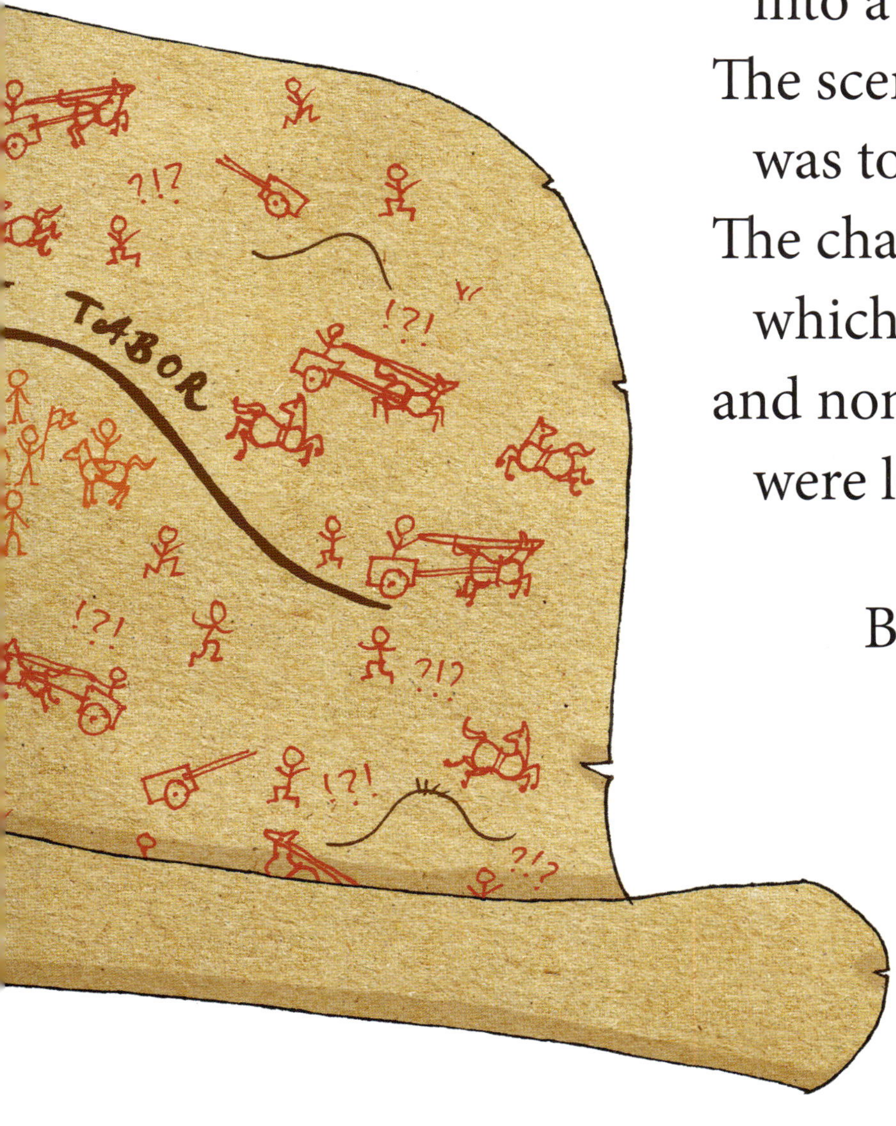

God threw the whole army
into a panic.
The scene which unfolded
was totally manic.
The chariots didn't know
which way to drive –
and none of the soldiers
were left alive.

But…

Sisera was,
  and he ran far away
to the home of some friends
  where he thought he might stay.
Heber was friends
  with Jabin, the King;
so Heber's wife Jael,
  welcomed Sisera in.
But God had a plan,
  and the plan was good –
He knew it would work,
  He knew that it would.
When God makes a plan,
  He uses His friends.
So God used Jael
  to make amends.

Jael was clever
and Jael was quick;
when Sisera turned up,
she thought of a trick.
She gave him some drink,
she gave him some rest,
and pretended to treat him
as some honoured guest.
Later that day
when Sisera slept,
she spotted her chance
at once – up she leapt!
She wasted no time;
oh yes, Jael made sure
that Sisera wouldn't be
mean anymore.

What a result!
They all were amazed,
and they sang to their God
in worship and praise –
"Lord God, you led
our leaders in war,
and everyone followed them
up Mount Tabor.
Listen, you rulers,
and listen, you kings:
It's God to whom everyone
dances and sings.
When God, the true King,
marches onto the plain,
there are earthquakes and thunder
and terrible rain.

is mean!
KiNG JaBiN

"Before, when we lived
in terror and fear,
when evil King Jabin
was ruling so near,
our God made a plan,
and the plan was good –
He knew it would work,
He knew that it would."

Deborah was wise
and Jael was brave.
Their mission in life?
God's people to save.
God used them and us too,
if we are His friends –
our story begins,
as this story ends.

The whole story can be found in the Bible. You could ask a grown-up to read it to you from Judges 4-5. But be careful – it is a bit gruesome.

Lucy Rycroft writes Christian parenting blog, Desertmum. Formerly a teacher and PGCE lecturer, she now divides her time between freelance writing, blogging and raising her kids. She writes regularly for 'Home for Good', is the author of 'Redeeming Advent', and this is her first book for children. Lucy lives in York with her husband and their four children.

lucyrycroft.com

Beth has always loved telling stories with pictures, something she has done since she was old enough to hold a crayon. She has studied art to postgraduate level and worked as an illustrator for many years. Over this time Beth has produced vibrant artwork for a wide range of clients from global publishing houses to individuals on independent commissions.

bethaulton.com